Dismantling
EV●LUTI●N
Made Easy

*A simple guide for taking
evolution apart, piece by piece*

Dr. Arv Edgeworth

Dismantling
EV●LUTI●N
Made Easy

A simple guide for taking
evolution apart, piece by piece

Dr. Arv Edgeworth

ISBN# 978-1-935075-15-8

Printed in the United States of America.

Printed by Calvary Publishing
A Ministry of Parker Memorial Baptist Church
1902 East Cavanaugh Road
Lansing, Michigan 48910
www.CalvaryPublishing.org

Contents

Acknowledgements

A special thanks to creationists David Bump, and Thomas Heinze for their much needed input in the writing of this book.

Introduction

The evolutionists' faith is founded upon four basic principles:

- *The Big Bang as the origin of the universe.*
- *Chemical evolution as the origin of life.*
- *The two mechanisms for the theory of evolution (mutations and natural selection).*
- *The fossil record as proof that evolution happened.*

This is where we will direct our focus in taking apart evolution. This is the foundation for everything else the evolutionist believes.

We will also share with you just three simple questions you should ask in each area of focus. This method is so easy you can write this information down on six index cards for help with memorization. We will also give you helps under "Digging Deeper" to deal with difficult questions, and give you a better understanding of the issues. However, this book is not intended to be a complete answer book. There are many other good books written that I would encourage you to purchase and read.

In His Service,
Dr. Arv Edgeworth

The Origin of the Universe

Good introductory question:
"Do you believe in the Big Bang?"

Our Focus: The Origin of the Universe (Space, time, matter, and energy). The evolutionists will claim that the universe began with an explosion from nothing.

> "The universe burst into something from absolutely nothing—zero, nada. And as it got bigger, it became filled with even more stuff that came from absolutely nowhere." (DISCOVER—April 2002)

The science books state it this way:

> "If you could run the life of the universe in reverse, like a film, you would see the universe contracting until it disappeared in a flash of light, leaving nothing. In the realm of the universe, nothing really means nothing. Not only matter and energy would disappear, but also space and time. However, physicists theorize that from this state of nothingness the universe began in a gigantic explosion about 16.5 billion years ago...the Big Bang." (HBJ General Science, 1989, p. 362)

> "...the observable universe could have evolved from an infinitesimal region*. It's then tempting to go one step further and speculate that the entire universe evolved from literally nothing." (Alan Guth & P. Steinhardt Scientific American, May 1984, p.128)

Some try to say that although nothing existed, a process known as vacuum fluctuation created what astrophysicists call a singularity, then from that singularity about the size of a dime, our universe was born. They still have the same problem. They start with nothing, but all of a sudden they have something. They still have to explain where the something came from.

Question #1

"Scientifically, can you have an explosion without energy?"

Question #2

"If there was no matter, what exploded?"

The First Law of Thermodynamics states: "Matter, and/or energy, cannot be created or destroyed." It is called the law of energy conservation. What that basically means is, matter or energy cannot come out of nothing.

> "The First Law has been the object of considerable thought since it was first introduced to the world by William Kelvin and Rudolph Clausius. It forbids a natural process from bringing something from nothing." (Dr. Robert Gauge, Origins and Destiny, 1986, p. 17)

Question # 3

"Scientifically, can something come from nothing?"

If someone tries to avoid this by arguing that space, time, matter, and energy have always existed, you simply refer to The Second Law of Thermodynamics which states: "Everything tends toward disorder." That means: Everything left to itself goes toward a state of disorder and decay, not order. It is called the law of energy deterioration. Everything would have reached maximum decay by now.

Isaac Asimov, an evolutionist himself, stated it this way:

> "Another way of stating the second law then is: 'The universe is constantly getting more disorderly!' Viewed that way, we can see the second law all about us. We have to work hard to straighten a room, but left to itself it becomes a mess again very quickly and very easily. Even if we never enter it, it becomes dusty and musty. How difficult to maintain houses, and machinery, and our bodies in perfect working order: how easy to let them deteriorate. In fact, all we have to do is nothing, and everything deteriorates, collapses, breaks down, wears out, all by itself – and that is what the second law is all about." (Smithsonian Institute Journal, June 1970, p. 6)

The Bible says: "…the heavens are the works of thine hands: They shall perish; but thou remainest; and they all shall wax old as doth a garment;" (Hebrews 1:10-11)

Reviewing the Questions:

- "*Scientifically, can you have an explosion without energy?*"
- "*If there was no matter, what exploded?*"

- *"Scientifically, can something come from nothing?"*

At this point some may just agree with you. But they may try to come up with an answer of some kind. After they have had their fun trying to answer the first three questions, just listen attentively, then just say: "That's interesting, let me ask you this..."

Please remember through all of this, they are not the enemy, Satan is. They are just a victim. You need to try to help them.

Digging Deeper
The Law of Cause and Effect

This is the most basic law of science. Every effect must have a cause. The cause will always be more complex and greater than the effect itself. Every event has a cause. The beginning of the universe was an event. Whatever the cause is, it will be greater than the effect itself. We live in a very orderly complex universe.

More Questions:

- *Where did the laws of the universe come from (gravity, inertia, etc.)?*
- *How did matter get so perfectly organized?*

- *Where did the energy and intelligence come from to do all the organizing?*
- *How did this explosion (or "expansion") cause order while every explosion ever observed and documented in recorded history caused only disorder and disarray?*
- *Is the entire universe really the result of an accidental explosion of nothing?*
- *How can simplicity become complexity?*
- *Attributing these things to evolution would violate known laws of science, does that make it a supernatural occurrence?*

Quotes

"I have little hesitation in saying that a sickly pall now hangs over the big bang theory." (Sir Fred Hoyle, astronomer, cosmologist, and mathematician, Cambridge University)

[The Big Bang] "... represents the instantaneous suspension of physical laws, the sudden, abrupt flash of lawlessness that allowed something to come out of nothing. It represents a true miracle-transcending physical principles..." (Paul Davies, The Edge of Infinity, New York: Simon and Schuster, 1981, p. 161)

The Bible's Answer

"In the beginning God created the heaven and the earth." (Genesis 1:1)

The word "beginning" has reference to time. The universe had a beginning, most people agree with that. Time has three dimensions: past, present, and future.

The word "heaven" has reference to space, that was the original firmament (Genesis 1:14). God was speaking a physical universe into existence. Space has three dimensions: length, height, and width.

The word "earth" has reference to matter. On the first day there was a whole universe, and one planet. But the planet was not formed to be inhabited yet (Isaiah 45:18). Over the first six days God was forming the earth to be inhabited. Matter has three dimensions: liquid, solid, and gas.

God also created a concept of time as He started planets spinning and orbiting. To create these things would take an enormous amount of energy. The Bible indicates that God has an inexhaustible supply. The first verse of the Bible tells us where space, time, matter, and energy all came from.

The Origin of Life

Transition questions:
"What about the beginning of life itself? Can life scientifically come from non-life?"

Our Focus: The Origin of Life. The evolutionists will claim that life came from non-life, from matter or dead chemicals.

Evolutionists call this chemical evolution. In the 1800s this was called spontaneous generation. Although they changed the terms, the meaning was exactly the same: life came from non-life through the right mixture of chemicals. Louis Pasteur and others proved that wrong through experimentation.

"Finally, in the mid-1800s, Louis Pasteur designed an experiment that disproved the spontaneous generation of microorganisms. From that time on, biogenesis, the idea that living organisms come only from other living organisms, became a cornerstone of biology." (Glencoe Biology, 2006, p. 381)

"Biologists have accepted the concept of biogenesis for more than 100 years." (Glencoe Biology, 2006, p. 382)

"Historically the point of view that life comes only from life has been so well established through the facts revealed by experiment that it is called the Law of Biogenesis." (Biology : a search for order in complexity, Moore and Slusher, 1984)

Question #1
"Isn't Biogenesis a law of science?"
In spite of this fact, students are taught the contrary: abiogenesis, life comes from non-life.

Question #2
"Is abiogenesis (life from non-life) scientific?" (Has it ever been observed?)

The evolutionists try to get around this:

"Scientists disagree about the details of the process that led to the origin of life. Most scientists, however, accept that under certain conditions, the basic molecules of life could have formed spontaneously through simple chemistry." (Holt Biology, Holt, Rinehart and Winston, 2006, p. 256)

Question #3
"If chemical evolution isn't happening today, how do we know it happened in the past?"

In 1953 two scientists by the name of Stanley Miller and Harold Urey performed an experiment in a laboratory for the purpose of trying to create life from chemicals. Under controlled conditions, drawing on years of experience, they designed the experiment to produce the best possible results, yet they only produced two amino acids, which actually bond with tar and are a toxic to life. Yet many claimed the experiment proved it could have happened.

Not only did Pasteur prove that life doesn't form from nutrient chemicals today, but the decades of evolutionists trying (and failing) to reproduce abiogenesis so far supports the contention that abiogenesis could never happen.

Reviewing the Questions:

- *"Isn't Biogenesis a law of science?"*
- *"Is abiogenesis (life from non-life) scientific? (Has it ever been observed?)"*
- *"If chemical evolution isn't happening today, how do we know it happened in the past?"*

Digging Deeper

The Law of Biogenesis

"There is no serious doubt that biogenesis is the rule, that life comes only from other life, that a cell, the unit of life, is always and exclusively the product or offspring of another cell" (Simpson and Beck , Life: An Introduction to Biology, 1965, p. 144)

Irreducible Complexity

We live in a world full of complexity. The smallest cell is more complex than the most complex machine man has invented, the space shuttle. Yet evolution demands that we go backwards in time to when things were less complex. But almost everything has to be that complex or it won't work.

More Questions:

- *If scientists could create life in a laboratory, how does that prove it doesn't take intelligence to create life?*

- *Which evolved first, plants, or the insects that pollinate them?*
- *Is the design and irreducible complexity of all living systems really the result of random chance?*
- *How can we explain the random development of the human eye, reproductive system, digestive tract, brain, heart and lungs?*

Quotes

"All of us who study the origin of life find that the more we look into it, the more we feel that it is too complex to have evolved anywhere. We believe as an article of faith that life evolved from dead matter on this planet. It is just that its complexity is so great, it is hard for us to imagine that it did." (Urey, Harold C., quoted in Christian Science Monitor, January 4, 1962, p. 4)

"Origin of Species Not addressed in 1859, and is still a mystery in 1998...Both the origin of life and the origin of the major groups of animals remains unknown."(Alfred G. Fisher, evolutionist Grolier Multimedia Encyclopedia 1998, fossil section)

The Mechanism for Evolution

Transition question:
"Have you ever thought about how evolution is supposed to work, through mutations and natural selection?"

Our Focus: The Mechanisms for Evolution. The evolutionists will claim that mutations and natural selection are the mechanisms that make evolution work.

Mechanism #1 - Mutations. What are mutations?

"The cell processes that copy genetic material and pass it from one generation to the next are usually accurate…however, changes in the DNA occasionally do occur… Any change in the DNA sequence is called a mutation." (Prentice Hall Biology, 2006, p. 301)

Evolution requires positive mutations

"In some rare cases, a gene mutation may have positive effects. An organism may receive a mutation that makes it faster or stronger; such a mutation may help an organism – and its offspring – better survive in its environment." (Prentice Hall Biology, 2006, p. 296)

What causes mutations?

"Mutations can be caused by errors in replication, transcription, cell division, or by external agents. (ex: radiation) Some mutations seem to just happen, perhaps as a mistake in base pairing during DNA replication. However, many mutations are caused by factors in the environment." (Prentice Hall Biology, 2006, p. 301)

"Any agent that can cause a change in DNA is called a mutagen. Mutagens include radiation, chemicals, and even high temperatures. Forms of radiation, such as X rays, cosmic rays, ultraviolet light, and nuclear radiation, are dangerous mutagens because the energy they contain can damage or break apart DNA." (Prentice Hall Biology, 2006, p. 301)

Almost all mutations are harmful.

"The mutation may produce a new trait or it may result in a protein that does not work correctly, resulting in structural or functional problems in cells and in the organism." (Prentice Hall Biology, 2006, p. 296)

Mutations are a series of information losing processes. This will not help you go from simple to complex! (See Dr. Lee Spetner's book, Not By Chance.)

Evolution requires a positive gain in new genetic information over time. Mutations cause a net loss in useful genetic information over time.

Question #1
"Aren't mutations almost always harmful?"

Question #2
"Don't mutations usually cause a net loss of information?"

Mechanism #2 - Natural Selection

"Natural selection is the mechanism by which evolution occurs." (Prentice Hall Biology, 2006, p. 18)

Natural Selection: The process in nature by which, according to Darwin's theory of evolution, only the organisms best adapted to their environment tend to survive and transmit their genetic characteristics in increasing numbers to succeeding generations while those less adapted tend to be eliminated. This is sometimes referred to as the "Survival of the Fittest."

No one disagrees with the "survival of the fittest." This was recognized by a creationist at least 24 years before Darwin wrote his book, however, he gave the credit to Father God instead of Mother Nature. Here's the problem. If you have a litter of nine kittens, and one of them is mutated, the mutated kitten is usually less healthy than the others. The eight healthy kittens are more likely to survive than the mutated one. Rather than helping life forms to turn into something else, natural selection usually helps them to remain the same!

Since the time of Darwin, evolutionists have believed that when a mutation causes an improvement, natural selection would preserve it, lifting plants and animals to ever higher levels. The problem is, almost all mutations are harmful.

Question # 3

"Wouldn't mutations usually be the least likely to survive?"

What we almost always see in nature, is that mutations make things worse, and natural selection will tend to eliminate the mutations. Mutations and natural selection are processes that work in opposition to the theory of evolution.

Evolution says organisms get better and more complex over time; mutations make things worse over time and less complex. Evolution requires changes to be passed on to future generations; natural selection usually prevents changes to be passed on.

Reviewing the Questions

- *"Aren't mutations almost always harmful?"*
- *"Don't mutations usually cause a net loss of information?"*
- *"Wouldn't mutations usually be the least likely to survive?"*

Digging Deeper

Every example of information requires four things:

- *A sender*
- *A receiver*
- *An information code*
- *An agreement between the sender and the receiver, concerning the code.*

This is always true. But evolutionists claim the most complex information source known to man, human DNA, didn't have a sender, but originated somehow from matter. They can give no examples of that happening in nature.

More Questions

- *How did cells with less information evolve into cells with much greater information?*
- *Aren't mutations moving in the wrong direction to support advancement of complexity?*
- *Do any structures in the cell resemble highly intricate machines designed by humans?*
- *Don't mutations just change information, not add new information?*
- *Where did the information come from in the first place?*

Quotes

"Mutations do not produce any kind of evolution."
(Pierre-Paul Grasse, Evolution of Living Organisms
1977, p. 88)

"It is easy enough to make up stories, of how one
form gave rise to another, and to find reasons why
the stages should be favoured by natural selection.
But such stories are not part of science, for there
is no way of putting them to the test." (Luther D
Sutherland, Darwin's Enigma, Master Books 1988,
p 89)

The Fossil Record

Transition question: *"Do you believe the fossil record proves evolution?"*

Our Focus: the Fossil Record. The evolutionist will claim that the fossil record proves evolution.

"Although the fossil record provides evidence that evolution occurred, the record is incomplete. Working with an incomplete fossil record is something like trying to put together a jigsaw puzzle with pieces missing. But after the puzzle is together, even with missing pieces, you will probably still understand the overall picture. Fossils are found throughout the world. As the fossil record becomes more complete, the sequences of evolution become clearer." (Glencoe Biology, 2006, p. 400)

"Most sedimentary rocks form in primarily horizontal layers with the younger layers closer to the surface. (Glencoe Biology, 2006, pg.372)

"Scientists use a variety of methods to determine the age of fossils. One method is a technique called relative dating. To understand relative dating, imagine yourself stacking newspapers at home. As each day's newspaper is added to the stack, the stack becomes taller. If the stack is left undisturbed, the newspapers at the bottom are older than ones at the top." (Glencoe Biology, 2006, p. 372)

Question # 1
"Is the actual fossil evidence anything like the chart?"

A chart, called the geologic column, is found in almost all science textbooks in some form. The chart shows the different layers of rock superimposed on top of each other, each representing a period of time, and each containing the fossils of life forms that supposedly lived during that time period. It is also referred to as the geologic timescale.

The evolutionists say the chart:

- *Represent the earth's presumed 4.6 billion year sequence of geologic ages.*
- *Records the evolutionary history of life on earth.*
- *Show simple organisms evolving into complex organisms.*
- *Show a gradual transition from one species to the next, finally into man.*

The creationists say:

- *The earth is only about 6,000 years old.*
- *Most of the rock layers and the fossils were formed by the Great Flood about 4,400 years ago.*

There are many problems with the geologic column (the chart used in the textbooks):

- *Circular reasoning is used. The rock will be dated by the fossil, and the fossil will be dated by the rock layer it is found in.*
- *Those twelve layers cannot be found together in that order anywhere in the world.*
- *Sometimes there are reversed layers (Older layers on top of younger).*
- *Sometimes fossils and artifacts will be found in the wrong layers.*

- *Sometimes fossils extend through many layers. (Polystrate fossils)*

Evolution Requires Multitudes of Transitional Fossils.

"Darwin realized that if his theory were true a large number of transitional fossils would be found in the fossil record. The lack of these transitional fossils was one of the points on which Darwin said his theory would be falsified." (Roger Patterson, Evolution Exposed, p. 114)

"The extreme rarity of transitional forms in the fossil record persists as the trade secret of paleontology, the evolutionary trees that adorn our textbooks have data only at the tips and nodes of their branches; the rest is inference, however reasonable, not the evidence of fossils." (Stephen J. Gould, Natural History, Vol. 86, pp. 22, 30)

Question # 2
"What about the absence of transitional fossils?"

"Paleontologists ever since Darwin have been searching (largely in vain) for the sequences of insensibly graded series of fossils that would stand as examples of the sort of wholesale transformation of species that Darwin envisioned as the natural product of the evolutionary process. Few saw any reason to demur- though it is a startling fact that,...

most species remain recognizably themselves, virtually unchanged throughout their occurrence in geological sediments of various ages." (Eldredge, Niles, "Progress in Evolution?" New Scientist, vol. 110, June 5, 1986, p. 55)

Question # 3
"Are there any fossils clearly in transition?"

That is a real problem for the theory of evolution, the lack of any real transitional fossils. If evolution were true, there should be millions of fossils that are in transition from one kind of creature to another. There should be fish that have partially formed legs, and reptiles with partially formed wings, and chimps that are partially human. Not only that, but we should see life forms still in transition today. But that type of change has never been observed in the fossil record, nor is it observable today.

When scientists come up with a hypothesis, they make predictions of what should be observable if their hypothesis is true. Darwin did that with his theory of evolution. He predicted transitional fossils would be found in the future when more fossils were available. None so far have been found. He said that would disprove his theory. So far it hasn't in the minds of most evolutionists.

Reviewing the Questions

- *"Is the actual fossil evidence anything like the chart?"*
- *"What about the absence of transitional fossils?"*
- *"Are there any fossils clearly in transition?"*

Digging Deeper

Fossils and rock layers do not speak for themselves—they must be interpreted. The way that you interpret evidence depends on the presuppositions you accept. The Bible offers a different set of presuppositions than naturalistic evolution.

The chart called the Geologic Column is actually made from combining pieces of the fossil record from all over the world. Geologists make many assumptions when trying to explain all of the fossils and rock layers.

The Actual Layers

The actual geologic column, representing the maximum thickness of all of the layers, would be over 90 miles thick, which occurs nowhere on earth. The only place it can actually be found is in the textbooks.

"If there were a column of sediments deposited continuously since the formation of the earth, the entire history of the planet could be reconstructed. Unfortunately no such column exists." (HBJ Earth Science 1989, p. 326)

"Roughly 1% of the earth's surface is covered by the 10 layers in succession, but these areas have not all been classified accurately based on the index fossils and other signs of life found in them." (Roger Patterson, Exposing Evolution, p. 123)

"2/3 of Earth's land surface has only 5 or fewer of the 10 geologic periods in place . . . 80-85% of Earth's land surface does not have even 3 geologic periods appearing in "correct" consecutive order... Since only a small percentage of the Earth's surface obeys even a significant portion of the geologic column, it becomes an overall exercise of gargantuan special pleading and imagination for the evolutionary uniformitarian paradigm to maintain that there ever were geologic periods." (J. Woodmorappe, CRS Quarterly, Vol. 18, No. 1, pp. 46-71)

"The fossils themselves are usually not directly dated. Instead, layers that contain datable igneous rocks above or below a fossil are used to estimate the age of the fossil." (Roger Patterson, Exposing Evolution, p, 113)

Human artifacts have been found in every rock strata, clear down into the Pre-Cambrian.

Different life forms that were supposed to represent index fossils for different ages have been found still alive.

The Bible has a better answer for the fossil record. It is called a great flood.

If you start out with a flood model, you can not only explain what is found in the fossil record, you can predict what will be found before you find it. (Like hammers and heavy objects in lower layers.)

Why do we find jellyfish and apple blossoms perfectly preserved in the fossil record? (Sudden deep burial)

Quotes

"The fossil record had caused Darwin more grief than joy. Nothing distressed him more than the Cambrian explosion, the coincident appearance of almost all complex organic designs…"(Gould, Stephen J., The Panda's Thumb, 1980, p. 238-239)

"The majority of major groups appear suddenly in the rocks, with virtually no evidence of transition from their ancestors." (Futuyma, D., Science on Trial: The Case for Evolution, 1983, p. 82)

"Despite the bright promise that paleontology provides a means of "seeing" evolution, it has presented some nasty difficulties for evolutionists the most notorious of which is the presence of "gaps" in the fossil record. Evolution requires intermediate forms between species and paleontology does not provide them. The gaps must therefore be a contingent feature of the record." (Kitts, David B., "Paleontology and Evolutionary Theory," Evolution, vol. 28, 1974, p. 467)

More Questions

- *Where are the billions of transitional fossils needed to prove evolution? Darwin said we would find them.*
- *What fossil evidence exists showing the evolution of one major kind of organism into another? We need a whole series.*
- *What evidence shows a transitional form with partially developed, nonfunctional features (such as 10% of a wing)?*

Hydrologic Sorting

The best explanation for the fossil record is hydrologic sorting. Things sort themselves out by density in water. The denser material sinks to the bottom first. If you take a glass jar and put several different kinds of soil in it, then fill the jar up with water and put the lid on tight, shake the jar up real good and set it down, it will sort itself by layers in about twenty minutes. The layers will be in straight lines and will resemble the layers in the Grand Canyon.

If we factor in body density, habitat, and the ability to survive, it will explain almost everything you find in the fossil record.

Understanding the Evolutionary Mindset

Some believe in evolution because it is all they have been taught. However, most evolutionists are just totally committed to their belief system, because the only alternative is special creation. There is no evidence that would prove evolution wrong to them. Stephen J. Gould said this: "There is a mystery as to how evolution occurs, but there is not a whole lot of doubt as to whether it occurs."

There is a great deal at stake here. If Somebody made the world, that Somebody would be the boss, and He would get to set the rules. If Nobody made it, we can be our own boss, and we get to set the rules. Acts 17:24 should settle that question: "God that made the world and all things therein, seeing that he is lord of heaven and earth…"

We all fall into one of two categories: We are either an honest seeker of truth, or we are a protector of a belief system. It shouldn't take you too long to figure out which category someone is in. If someone is willingly stupid (2 Peter 3:5), I wouldn't spend a lot of time with them. I would give them a few things to think about, but then move on. That's what the Bible means by not casting your pearls before swine (Matthew 7:6).

They have an Atheistic Anti-Christian agenda. In 1881 Charles Lyell said his goal was to "free the science from Moses." (Life Letters and Journals', published by John Murray 1881)

In 1880, in reply to a correspondent, Charles Darwin wrote:

> "I am sorry to have to inform you that I do not believe in the Bible as a divine revelation, and therefore not in Jesus Christ as the Son of God." "I can indeed hardly see how anyone ought to wish Christianity to be true; for if so, the plain language of the text seems to show that the men who do not believe, and this would include my Father, Brother, and almost all my best friends, will be everlastingly punished. And this is a damnable doctrine…"

Issac Asimov said, "It seems to me that God is a

convenient invention of the human mind."

Richard Dawkins said:

"Faith is the great cop-out, the great excuse to evade the need to think and evaluate evidence. Faith is belief in spite of, even perhaps because of, the lack of evidence." "Religious people split into three main groups when faced with science. I shall label them the 'know-nothings', the 'know-alls', and the 'no-contests.'"

"Christianity has fought, still fights, and will fight science to the desperate end over evolution, because evolution destroys utterly and finally the very reason Jesus' earthly life was supposedly made necessary. Destroy Adam and Eve and the original sin, and in the rubble you will find the sorry remains of the son of god [sic]. Take away the meaning his death. If Jesus was not the redeemer who died for our sins, and this is what evolution means, then Christianity is nothing!" (G. Richard Bozarth, "The Meaning of Evolution," The American Atheist, Vol. 20, No. 2, February 1978, p. 30)

If I really didn't believe that God existed, I would be amused by statements about Him. Most evolutionists fly into a rage. That is because they have set their heart against Him.

The Three Main Tactics Of Evolutionists

1. Redefining the Terms

Evolutionists will try to change the definitions so they will only fit evolution. They try to define science as "change." They say this: "That's what science is all about, change." No, actually, the word science means "to know," not "to change." Science is all about a search for the truth. "Evolution" is all about change, but that is not the same thing.

Another example is, they will make this claim: "There are no scientists that do not believe in evolution. Therefore, if someone doesn't believe in evolution they are not a true scientist." It doesn't matter what college they graduated from, or what degrees they hold, or even if they once believed in evolution. As soon as someone doubts evolution, they are not a true scientist, and shouldn't be trusted.

They also make the claim that evolution is science and creation is just a religious belief. The idea that science cannot accept a creationist perspective is a denial of scientific history. What about men such as Bacon, Galileo, Kepler, Newton, etc.? According to the evolutionary thinking of today, these men should not be considered real scientists.

Johannes Kepler [1571-1630] Astronomy/ Laws of Planetary Motion— He stated that in his astronomy research, he was merely "thinking God's thoughts after Him."

Sir Isaac Newton [1642-1727] Mathematician, Physicist Inventor of calculus - Law of universal gravitation—"This thing [a scale model of our solar system] is but a puny imitation of a much grander system whose laws you know, and I am not able to convince you that this mere toy is without a designer and maker;"

Louis Pasteur [1822-1895] Father of Microbiology, developed "pasteurization" - "The more I study nature, the more I stand amazed at the work of the Creator." "Science brings men nearer to God."

Lord Kelvin [1824-1907] Physicist, Laws of Thermodynamics, Absolute temperature scale, inventor—"With regard to the origin of life, science... positively affirms creative power."

Another example is telling the students they should only look for natural answers to their questions, thus ruling out anything that is supernatural.

"Science requires repeatable observations and testable hypotheses. These standards restrict science to a search for natural causes for natural phenomena." (Biology: Exploring Life, Prentice Hall 2006, p. 38)

Once a scientist (or anyone else), considers facts through a preconceived filter, the true quest for knowledge stops. The mistake comes in assuming your hypothesis is true, and looking at all evidence in that light. When that occurs, it fails to be science.

In a biblical worldview, if conclusions contradict the truth revealed in Scripture, the conclusions are rejected.

The same thing happens in naturalistic science. Any conclusion that does not have a naturalistic explanation is rejected.

The students are not taught to look for the best answers, or the answers that best fit the evidence, just the answers that are purely naturalistic.

Look at this statement:

> "Even if all the data point to an intelligent designer, such an hypothesis is excluded from science because it is not naturalistic." (Dr. Scott Todd, Kansas State University, Nature 401 (6752):423, Sept. 30, 1999)

2. Using Wishful Speculations

Evolutionists will use such "fuzzy terms" as: "Could have ... Might have ... Probably did ... We believe ... We think ..."

> "What was early Earth like? Some scientists suggest that it was probably very hot. The energy from col-

liding meteorites could have heated its surface, while both the compression of minerals and the decay of radioactive materials heated its interior. Volcanoes might have frequently spewed lava and gases, relieving some of the pressure in Earth's hot interior... Although it probably contained no free oxygen, water vapor and other gases, such as carbon dioxide and nitrogen, most likely were present. If ancient Earth's atmosphere was like this, you would not have survived in it." (Glencoe Biology: The Dynamics of Life 2006, p. 369)

"Scientists hypothesize that two developments must have preceded the appearance of life on Earth. First, simple organic molecules, or molecules that contain carbon, must have formed. Then these molecules must have become organized into complex organic molecules such as proteins, carbohydrates, and nucleic acids that are essential to life... Remember that Earth's early atmosphere probably contained no free oxygen. Instead, the atmosphere was probably composed of water vapor, carbon dioxide, nitrogen, and perhaps methane and ammonia. Many scientists have tried to explain how these substances could have joined together and formed the simple organic molecules that are found in all organisms today." (Glencoe Biology: The Dynamics of Life 2006, p. 382)

These are statements of faith. They "know" it must have happened somehow, so they make these "fuzzy" statements and are happy to leave it that way.

3. Making Unsupported Claims

Evolutionists often claim to have more evidence than they do (bluffing). For example: "The fossil record proves evolution." "We know humans evolved from apes."

"Evolutionists claim (without any basis in reality) that our entire world of precise design exists as it does today because of certain impersonal, chance events. By chance the universe exploded into existence, and by chance the earth had just the right conditions for primeval life. By chance the first living cell came into being out of a primordial pool of organic nutrients. By chance also, this first living cell continued to evolve and gave rise over millions and billions of years to the whole vast array of plants, animals, and people around us! Evolutionism, like ancient paganism, is a world of chance, not the scientific world of law, order, and design." (Evolution: A Retreat from Science, Biology: God's Living Creation. A Beka Publishing, 1986 p. 367)

"When scientists attribute instrumental power to chance they have left the realm of reason, they have left the domain of science. They have turned to pulling rabbits out of hats. They have turned to fantasy. Insert the idea of chance, and all scientific investigation ultimately becomes chaotic and absurd." (John MacArthur, The Battle for the Beginning, Word Publishing, 2001 p. 39)

Evolution, Creation, and Beginnings

Proponents of both Creation and Evolution say space, time, matter, and energy came into existence from nothing. Creationists just do not believe that nothing can do it completely by itself without help. For everything to come into existence from nothing takes a supernatural event.

"Through faith we understand that the worlds were framed by the word of God, so that things which are seen were not made of things which do appear." (Hebrews 11:3)

Both sides also believe that life came into existence from dead matter. However, creationists don't believe that will just happen naturally without a supernatural agent involved.

Historical and Operational Science

The word "Evolution" has many meanings, only one of which is observable science.

- *Cosmic evolution - the origin of time, space, matter, and energy (Big Bang)*
- *Chemical evolution - the origin of higher elements from hydrogen*
- *Stellar and planetary evolution - the origin of stars and planets*
- *Organic evolution - the origin of life*
- *Macro-evolution - the origin of major kinds*
- *Micro-evolution - the variations within kinds*

Which one is observable? (Only the last one)

The Result of an Evolutionary Worldview
- *Man has no hope for his own future.*
- *One of the races of humans must be superior to the rest.*
- *Man is just an animal.*
- *Inferiors should be eliminated for the good of the species.*
- *Protection of the world and environment is the ultimate duty of man as the highest evolved animal.*
- *Might makes right.*

Quotes

"The more one studies paleontology, the more certain one becomes that evolution is based on faith alone; exactly the same sort of faith which it is necessary to have when one encounters the great mysteries of religion." (More, Louis T., "The Dogma of Evolution," Princeton University Press: Princeton NJ, 1925, Second Printing, p.160)

"I am convinced, moreover, that Darwinism, in whatever form, is not in fact a scientific theory, but a pseudo-metaphysical hypothesis decked out in scientific garb. In reality the theory derives its support not from empirical data or logical deductions of a scientific kind but from the circumstance that it happens to be the only doctrine of biological origins that can be conceived with the constricted worldview to which a majority of scientists no doubt subscribe." (Wolfgang, Smith, "The Universe is Ultimately to be Explained in Terms of a Metacosmic Reality" in Margenau and Varghese (eds.), Cosmos, Bios, Theos, p. 113)

"Life, even in bacteria, is too complex to have occurred by chance." (Rubin, Harry, "Life, Even in Bacteria, Is Too Complex to Have Occurred by Chance" in Margenau and Varghese (eds.), Cosmos, Bios, Theos, p. 203)

"Often a cold shudder has run through me, and I have asked myself whether I may have not devoted myself to a fantasy." (Charles Darwin, The Life and Letters of Charles Darwin, 1887, Vol. 2, p. 229)

"Evolutionism is a fairy tale for grown-ups. This theory has helped nothing in the progress of science. It is useless." (Professor Louis Bouroune, former President of the Biological Society of Strasbourg and Director of the Strasbourg Zoological Museum, later Director of Research at the French National Centre of Scientific Research, as quoted in The Advocate, March 8, 1984)

"Scientists who go about teaching that evolution is a fact of life are great con-men, and the story they are telling may be the greatest hoax ever. In explaining evolution we do not have one iota of fact." (Dr. T.N. Tahmisian. Atomic Energy Commission, The Fresno Bee, August 20, 1959)

"A five million year old piece of bone that was thought to be the collarbone of a humanlike creature is actually part of a dolphin rib... The problem with a lot of anthropologists is that they want so much to find a hominid that any scrap of bone becomes a hominid bone." (Dr. Tim White, anthropologist, University of California, Berkeley, New Scientist, April 28, 1983)

"One is forced to conclude that many scientists and technologists pay lip-service to Darwinian theory only because it supposedly excludes a Creator." (Dr. Michael Walker, Senior Lecturer in Anthropology, Sydney University, quoted in Quadrant, Oct., 1982)

"The irony is devastating. The main purpose of Darwinism was to drive every last trace of an incredible God from biology. But the theory replaces God with an even more incredible deity - omnipotent chance." (T. Rosazak, "Unfinished Animal," 1975, pp. 101-102)

Closing the deal

Here is how you make the transition from creation – evolution to *"What must I do to be saved?"*

There are 3 basic reasons I scientifically reject the theory of evolution:

1. The laws of science are in disagreement with it.

- *The first and second laws of thermodynamics*
- *The law of biogenesis*
- *The law of cause and effect*

2. The two mechanisms actually work against it.

3. I believe there is a better answer for the fossil record that fits the evidence better. Castastrophism, like the scientists in the mid-1800s believed.

I think I know why so many still believe in it though. You want to know why I think most people believe in evolution, and reject creation?

They are afraid if creation is true, they will have to stand before God and be judged some day. Did you know that isn't something people have to be afraid of?

What if I could show you how to take the fear out of dying and future judgment? Would you be interested?

(This is where you switch to the other simple plan, the simple plan of salvation that you feel most comfortable with.)

I would recommend putting this simple plan on

index cards. I would list the FOCUS and any introductory questions on the front, and put the three questions on the back. Practice with the index cards until it becomes natural for you. (See end of book) Also study the DIGGING DEEPER section so you will be prepared for other issues that might come up. I would also recommend purchasing other good books on the Creation versus Evolution issue. I hope this book gives you direction and topics to focus on, and simple questions to ask to put things in perspective. As time goes on you may develop other questions of your own that would work equally as well.

Getting Technical

For those who want to look at the more technical aspects of each chapter, this section is for you.

Chapter 1

The Big Bang

The evolutionists start out with the assumption that natural forces are all that have ever acted upon the universe. They assume that if there is a God (although most reject that idea), He has not intervened in any supernatural way. This leaves them with no other possible explanation than to start with something like a Big Bang.

NASA explains it this way: "The universe was created sometime between 10 billion and 20 billion years ago from a cosmic explosion that hurled matter, and in all directions." (http://liftoff.msfc.nasa.gov/academy/universe/b_bang.html)

UC Berkeley explains it this way: "The big bang theory states that at some time in the distant past there was nothing. A process known as vacuum fluctuation created what astrophysicists call a singularity. From that singularity, which was about the size of a dime, our Universe was born." (http://cosmology.berkeley.edu/Education/IUP/Big_Bang_Primer.html)

The Second Law of Thermodynamics states: "Everything tends toward disorder." What that basically means is: Everything left to itself goes toward a state of disorder and decay, not order. It is called the law of energy deterioration.

If someone believes in the Big Bang theory where matter and energy has always existed, ask them this:

Question # 1

"Doesn't the second law of thermodynamics state that matter and energy are both deteriorating?"

Even if you could get something out of nothing, it would immediately start to decay.

Question # 2
"How could matter and energy always have existed?"

Question # 3
"Why haven't they already reached maximum decay?"

Most evolutionists today agree that the universe did have a beginning, so you will possibly not have to use the second set of questions listed above,

Besides conflicting with the Laws of Thermodynamics, the Big Bang Theory also contradicts the Law of Conservation of Angular Momentum.

If anything is spinning fast, anything that flies off from it will be spinning in the same direction. There are planets and moons that are spinning in opposite directions at the same time (this is called "Retrograde Motion"). It shouldn't be that way if the Big Bang theory is true. Venus, Uranus, and Pluto are spinning backwards in relation to the other planets in our own solar system.

Mitch Cervinka, M.A. Mathematics:
Evolution Is Not Science
There are several fundamental characteristics that identify a field of study as being "scientific."

Genuine science is objective and invites scrutiny and investigation. It does not ridicule the critics of its conclusions, but instead silences their criticisms by setting forth the evidence from which those conclusions are drawn.

Genuine science seeks the truth that explains the observed evidence. It does not prejudice the investigation by ruling out, from the start, hypotheses that may very well provide the best explanation for the observed evidence.

Genuine science rejects any hypothesis that consistently fails to fit observed scientific evidence. It does not persistently assume that the fault lies in the evidence rather than in the hypothesis itself.

More Quotes:

"Since matter and antimatter are equivalent in all respects but that of electromagnetic charge oppositeness, any force [the Big Bang] that would create one should have to create the other, and the universe should be made of equal quantities of each. This is a dilemma. Theory tells us there should be antimatter out there, and observation refuses to back it up." (Isaac Asimov, Asimov's New Guide to Science, p. 343)

"We are pretty sure from our observations that the universe today contains matter, but very little if any antimatter." (Victor Weisskopf, "The Origin of the Universe," American Scientist, 71, p. 479)

"Attempts to explain both the expansion of the universe and the condensation of galaxies must be largely contradictory so long as gravitation is the only force field under consideration. For if the expansive kinetic energy of matter is adequate to give universal expansion against the gravitational field, it is adequate to prevent local condensation under gravity, and vice versa. That is why, essentially, the formation of galaxies is passed over with little comment in most systems of cosmology."(*F. Hoyle and *T. Gold, quoted in *D.B. Larson, Universe in Motion, 1984, p. 8)

"To express all this, we can say: 'Energy can be transferred from one place to another, or transformed from one form to another, but it can be neither created nor destroyed.' Or we can put it another way: 'The total quantity of energy in the universe is constant.' This law is considered the most powerful and most fundamental generalization about the universe that scientists have ever been able to make." (Asimov, Isaac, "In the Game of Energy and Thermodynamics You Can't Even Break Even," Smithsonian Institute Journal, June 1970, p. 6)

"What is a big deal—the biggest deal of all—is how you get something out of nothing...Don't let the cosmologists try to kid you on this one. They have not got a clue either—despite the fact that they are doing a pretty good job of convincing themselves and others that this is really not a problem. 'In the beginning,' they will say, 'there was nothing—no time, space, matter or energy. Then there was a quantum fluctuation from which ' Whoa! Stop right there. You see what I mean? First there is nothing, then there is something. And the cosmologists try to bridge the two with a quantum flutter, a tremor of uncertainty that sparks it all off. Then they are away and before you know it, they have pulled a hundred billion galaxies out of their quantum hats...You cannot fudge this by appealing to quantum mechanics. Either there is nothing to begin with, in which case there is no quantum vacuum, no pre-geometric dust, no time in which anything can happen, no physical laws that can effect a change from nothingness into somethingness; or there is something, in which case that needs explaining." (Darling, David, "On Creating Something from Nothing," New Scientist, vol. 151, September 14, 1996, p. 49)

"Evolution means the creation of larger and larger islands of order at the expense of ever greater seas of disorder in the world. There is not a single biologist or physicist who can deny this central truth. Yet, who is willing to stand up in a classroom or before a public forum and admit it?"(Rifkin, Jeremy, Entropy: A New World View, New York: Viking Press, 1980, p. 55)

Chapter 2
Life From Non-Life
"The idea of life coming from nonlife, spontaneous generation, was a popular idea from the time of the Greek philosophers." (Evolution Exposed, by Roger Patterson, p. 139)

The Origin of Life: The Early Ideas
"In the past, the ideas that decaying meat produced maggots, mud produced fishes, and grain produced mice were reasonable explanations for what people observed occurring in their environment. After all, they saw maggots appear on meat and young mice appear in sacks of grain. Such observations led people to believe in spontaneous generation – the idea that nonliving material can produce life." (Glencoe Biology, 2006, p. 380)

The Law of Biogenesis
"As David Kirk correctly stated: By the end of the nineteenth century there was general agreement that life cannot arise from the nonliving under conditions that now exist upon our planet. The dictum 'All life from preexisting life' became the dogma of modern biology, from which no reasonable man could be expected to dissent...The experiments that formed the ultimate basis of this law were first carried out by such men as Francesco Redi (1688) and Lazarro Spallanzani (1799) in Italy, Louis Pasteur (1860) in France, and Rudolph Virchow (1858) in Germany. It was Virchow who documented that cells do not

arise from amorphous matter, but instead come only from preexisting cells. The Encyclopaedia Britannica states concerning Virchow that "His aphorism 'omnis cellula e cellula' (every cell arises from a preexisting cell) ranks with Pasteur's 'omne vivum e vivo' (every living thing arises from a preexisting living thing) among the most revolutionary generalizations of biology" (Bert Thompson, The Bible and the Laws of Science: The Law of Biogenesis, 1973, p. 35)

"In recent years, however, some evolutionists have suggested that what is commonly referred to as the 'law' of biogenesis is not a 'law' at all, but only a 'principle' or 'theory' or 'dictum.' This new nomenclature is being suggested by evolutionists because they have come to the stark realization of the implications of the law of biogenesis—not because contradictions or exceptions to the law have been discovered. It is of interest to note that in nineteenth-century science texts, biogenesis was spoken of as a law. But, of late, that term has been replaced by new terms that are intended to 'soften' the force of biogenesis upon evolutionary concepts." (Bert Thompson, The Bible and the Laws of Science: The Law of Biogenesis, 1973, p. 35)

DNA Crams Information into a Tiny Space:

If the first cell arose from chemicals without a Creator, how could it have come up with the most efficient container of information imaginable?

Werner Gitt, an information scientist, puts it this way:

> "DNA molecules contain the highest known packing density of information. This exceedingly brilliant storage method reaches the limit of the physically possible." (Werner Gitt, In the Beginning Was Information, 1997, p. 195)

Does not the fact that DNA started out with the perfect solution for getting the greatest amount of information in the smallest space indicate that it had a very exceptional designer?

> "If they eventually make a computer as small as a cell with a huge information storage capacity like DNA, and I scoff and claim: 'You didn't do that! It just came about by accident,' they will rightly consider me a fool." (Thomas F. Heinze, How Life Began, 2002, p. 107)

Quotes

Michael Behe, a renowned microbiologist at Lehigh University, gives an example of irreducible complexity:

> "Cilia are hairlike organelles on the surfaces of many animal and lower plant cells that serve to move fluid over the cell's surface or to "row" single cells through a fluid...Cilia are composed of at least a half dozen

proteins: alpha-tubulin, beta-tubulin, dynein, nexin, spoke protein, and a central bridge protein. These combine to perform one task, ciliary motion, and all of these proteins must be present for the cilium to function. If the tubulins are absent, then there are no filaments to slide; if the dynein is missing, then the cilium remains rigid and motionless; if nexin or the other connecting proteins are missing, then the axoneme falls apart when the filaments slide…What we see in the cilium, then, is not just profound complexity, but also irreducible complexity on the molecular scale. Recall that by "irreducible complexity" we mean an apparatus that requires several distinct components for the whole to work. My mousetrap must have a base, hammer, spring, catch, and holding bar, all working together, in order to function. Similarly, the cilium, as it is constituted, must have the sliding filaments, connecting proteins, and motor proteins for function to occur. In the absence of any one of those components, the apparatus is useless." (M. Behe: "Molecular Machines: Experimental Support for the Design Inference")

"If living matter is not, then, caused by the interplay of atoms, natural forces and radiation, how has it come into being? I think, however, that we must go further than this and admit that the only acceptable explanation is creation. I know that this is anathema to physicists, as indeed it is to me, but we must not reject a theory that we do not like if the experimental evidence supports it." (H.J. Lipson, F.R.S. Professor of Physics, University of Manchester, UK, "A physicist looks at evolution" Physics Bulletin, 1980, vol 31, p. 138)

"An honest man, armed with all the knowledge available to us now, could only state that, in some sense, the origin of life appears at the moment to be almost a miracle. So many are the conditions which would have had to have been satisfied to get it going. But this should not be taken to imply that there are good reasons to believe that it could not have started on the earth by a perfectly reasonable sequence of fairly ordinary chemical reactions. The plain fact is that the time available was too long, the many microenvironments on the earth's surface too diverse, the various chemical possibilities too numerous and our own knowledge and imagination too feeble to allow us to be able to unravel exactly how it might or might not have happened such a long time ago, especially as we have no experimental evidence from that era to check our ideas against." (Francis Crick, Life Itself, Its Origin and Nature, 1981, p. 88)

"There is still a tremendous problem with the sudden diversification of multi-cellular life. There is no question about that. That's a real phenomenon." (Niles Eldredge, quoted in Darwin's Enigma: Fossils and Other Problems by Luther D. Sunderland, Master Book Publishers, Santee, California, 1988, p. 45)

"The likelihood of the formation of life from inanimate matter is one to a number with 40,000 noughts after it ... It is big enough to bury Darwin and the whole theory of evolution ... if the beginnings of life were not random, they must therefore have been the product of purposeful intelligence." (Sir Fred Hoyle, astronomer, cosmologist and mathematician, Cambridge University)

"One has only to contemplate the magnitude of this task to concede that the spontaneous generation of a living organism is impossible. Yet here we are—as a result, I believe, of spontaneous generation."(Wald, George, "The Origin of Life," in The Physics and Chemistry of Life, Simon & Schuster, 1955, p. 9)

"If there were a basic principle of matter which somehow drove organic systems toward life, its existence should easily be demonstrable in the laboratory. One could, for instance, take a swimming bath to represent the primordial soup. Fill it with any chemicals of a non-biological nature you please. Pump any gases over it, or through it, you please, and shine any kind of radiation on it that takes your fancy. Let the experiment proceed for a year and see how many of those 2,000 enzymes [proteins produced by living cells] have appeared in the bath. I will give the answer, and so save the time and trouble and expense of actually doing the experiment. You would find nothing at all, except possibly for a tarry sludge composed of amino acids and other simple organic chemicals. How can I be so confident of this statement? Well, if it were otherwise, the experiment would long since have been done and would be well-known and famous throughout the world. The cost of it would be trivial compared to the cost of landing a man on the Moon." (Hoyle, Sir Fred, The Intelligent Universe, New York: Holt, Rinehart & Winston, 1983, pp. 20-21)

"But the most sweeping evolutionary questions at the level of biochemical genetics are still unanswered. How the genetic code first appeared and then evolved and, earlier than that, how life itself originated on earth remain for the future to resolve, though dim and narrow pencils of illumination already play over them. The fact that in all organisms living today the processes both of replication of the DNA and of the effective translation of its code require highly precise enzymes and that, at the same time the molecular structures of those same enzymes are precisely specified by the DNA itself, poses a remarkable evolutionary mystery.... Did the code and the means of translating it appear simultaneously in evolution? It seems almost incredible that any such coincidence could have occurred, given the extraordinary complexities of both sides and the requirement that they be coordinated accurately for survival. By a pre-Darwinian (or a skeptic of evolution after Darwin) this puzzle would surely have been interpreted as the most powerful sort of evidence for special creation." (Haskins, Caryl P., "Advances and Challenges in Science in 1970," American Scientist, vol. 59, May/June 1971, p. 305)

Points to consider

- *A mixture of left-handed and right-handed amino acids is a poison to life.*
- *All biological proteins (all life) contain 100% left-handed amino acids.*
- *When a living organism dies, the natural property of amino acids is to revert to a mixture (left-handed and right-handed).*
- *When a solution of left-handed amino acids is left alone, the amino acids slowly alter until the solution becomes approximately a mixture of 50/50 right-handed and left-handed amino acids.*

Chapter 3
Mutations and Natural Selection

Evolution not only requires positive or beneficial mutations, it requires a series of beneficial mutations that add complex new parts. And even if that could happen, it needs to have them all accumulate before all the negative mutations kill off the population.

Adaptations indicate purpose and direction.

Can evolution have purpose and direction? Doesn't an adaptation have to appear before natural selection can act upon it? If evolution is not directed by a purpose, would it be safe to say that human existence is purposeless?

Quotes

> "Natural selection is incompetent to account for the incipient stages of useful structures." (George Mivart in On the Genesis of Species)

> "The essence of Darwinism lies in a single phrase: natural selection is the creative force of evolutionary change. No one denies that natural selection will play a negative role in eliminating the unfit. Darwinian theories require that it create the fit as well." (Stephen Jay Gould, Professor of Geology and Paleontology, Harvard University, "The return of hopeful monsters." Natural History, vol. LXXXVI, 6, June-July 1977, p. 28)

> "That a mindless, purposeless, chance process such as natural selection, acting on the sequels of recombinant DNA or random mutation, most of which are injurious or fatal, could fabricate such complexity and organization as the vertebrate eye, where each component part must carry out its own distinctive task in a harmoniously functioning optical unit, is inconceivable. The absence of transitional forms between the invertebrates retina and that of the vertebrates poses another difficulty. Here there is a great gulf fixed which remains inviolate with no seeming likelihood of ever being bridged. The total picture

speaks of intelligent creative design of an infinitely high order." (H.S.Hamilton (MD) The Retina of the Eye - An Evolutionary Road Block.)

"Nowhere was Darwin able to point to one bona fide case of natural selection having actually generated evolutionary change in nature...Ultimately, the Darwinian theory of evolution is no more nor less than the great cosmogenic myth of the twentieth century." (Michael Denton, Evolution: A Theory in Crises, Bethesda, Maryland: Adler & Adler, 1986, pp. 62, 358)

Chapter 4
Quotes

"Contrary to what most scientists write, the fossil record does not support the Darwinian theory of evolution because it is this theory (there are several) which we use to interpret the fossil record. By doing so, we are guilty of circular reasoning if we then say the fossil record supports this theory." (West, R., Kansas State Univ., Paleontology and Uniformitarianism, Compass 45:216, 1968, p. 105)

"The fossils themselves are usually not directly dated. Instead, layers that contain datable igneous rocks above or below a fossil are used to estimate the age of the fossil." (Roger Patterson – Exposing Evolution, p. 113)

The Layers are seldom in the right order.

Lewis Overthrust: In Montana, "Pre-Cambrian" rocks lie on top of "Cretaceous" rocks that are supposed to be 500 million years younger. This contradiction is explained by a thrust in which a piece of land 350 miles wide and six miles thick (about 10,000 square miles in area) picked itself up and slid 40 miles on top of the "Cretaceous" strata.

Franklin Overthrust: In Texas, rocks 450 million years old lie on top of rocks 130 million years old.

Mythen Peak: The Mythen Peak in the Alps has rocks 200 million years old on top of rocks 60 million years old. The thrust is believed to have pushed all the way from Africa to Switzerland.

Glarus Overthrust: In Switzerland, rocks 180 million years old lie on top of rocks 60 million years old. Rock a mile in thickness is believed to have been moved 21 miles. The order is Eocene (youngest) at the bottom, Jurassic (older) next, then Permian (much older) on top. This would be an impossible order if the evolutionary geological time scale were true.

Heart Mountain Thrust: In Wyoming, about 2,000 square miles of rock supposedly 300 million years old rests on top of rock 60 million years old.

Matterhorn: The Matterhorn in the Alps has supposedly been thrust from 60 miles away resulting in "younger" rocks on top of "older" rocks.

At a location known as West Crazy Cat Canyon near El Paso, Texas, scientists found massive Ordovician limestones on top of Cretaceous strata. Evolutionists suppose the Ordovician period is the age of sea life, and Cretaceous is the age of the dinosaurs.

More Quotes:

Transitional Fossils

"This regular absence of transitional forms is not confined to mammals, but is an almost universal phenomenon, as has long been noted by paleontologists. It is true of almost all orders of all classes of animals, both vertebrate and invertebrate. A fortiori, it is also true of the classes, and of the major animal phyla, and it is apparently also true of analogous categories of plants." (G. G. Simpson, Tempo and Mode in Evolution, New York, Columbia University Press, 1944, p. 107)

"Species that were once thought to have turned into others have been found to overlap in time with these alleged descendants. In fact, the fossil record does not convincingly document a single transition from one species to another." (Stanley, S.M., The New Evolutionary Timetable: Fossils, Genes, and the Origin of Species, 1981, p. 95)

"Indeed, it is the chief frustration of the fossil record that we do not have empirical evidence for sustained trends in the evolution of most complex morphological adaptations." (Gould, Stephen J. and Eldredge, Niles, "Species Selection: Its Range and Power," 1988, p. 19)

"The majority of major groups appear suddenly in the rocks, with virtually no evidence of transition from their ancestors." (Futuyma, D., Science on Trial: The Case for Evolution, 1983, p. 82)

"But fossil species remain unchanged throughout most of their history and the record fails to contain a single example of a significant transition." (Woodroff, D.S., Science, vol. 208, 1980, p. 716)

"It is as though they [fossils] were just planted there, without any evolutionary history. Needless to say this appearance of sudden planting has delighted creationists. ...Both schools of thought (Punctuationists and Gradualists) despise so-called scientific creationists equally, and both agree that the major gaps are real, that they are true imperfections in the fossil record. The only alternative explanation of the sudden appearance of so many complex animal types in the Cambrian era is divine creation and (we) both reject this alternative." (Dawkins, Richard, The Blind Watchmaker, W.W. Norton & Company, New York, 1996, p. 229-230)

"In any case, no real evolutionist, whether gradualist or punctuationist, uses the fossil record as evidence in favour of the theory of evolution as opposed to special creation." (Ridley, Mark, "Who doubts evolution?" "New Scientist," vol. 90, 25 June 1981, p. 831)

"The geological record has provided no evidence as to the origin of the fishes." (Norman, J., A History of Fishes, 1963, p. 298)

"None of the known fishes is thought to be directly ancestral to the earliest land vertebrates." (Stahl, B., Vertebrate History: Problems in Evolution, Dover Publications, Inc., NY, 1985, p. 148)

"Undeniably, the fossil record has provided disappointingly few gradual series. The origins of many groups are still not documented at all." (Futuyma, D., Science on Trial: The Case for Evolution, 1983, p. 190-191)

"[There is not] enough evidence from fossil material to take theorising out of the realms of fantasy." (New Scientist, August 1972, p. 259)

A significant percentage of every geologic period's rocks does not overlie rocks of the next geologic period . . . Some percentage of every geologic period rests directly upon Precambrian "basement."(J. Woodmorappe, CRS Quarterly, Vol. 18, No. 1, pp. 46-71)

Chapter 5
Quotes

"I am convinced, moreover, that Darwinism, in whatever form, is not in fact a scientific theory, but a pseudo-metaphysical hypothesis decked out in scientific garb. In reality the theory derives its support not from empirical data or logical deductions of a scientific kind but from the circumstance that it happens to be the only doctrine of biological origins that can be conceived with the constricted worldview to which a majority of scientists no doubt subscribe." (Wolfgang, Smith, "The Universe is Ultimately to be Explained in Terms of a Metacosmic Reality" in Margenau and Varghese (eds.), Cosmos, Bios, Theos, p. 113)

"Life, even in bacteria, is too complex to have occurred by chance." (Rubin, Harry, "Life, Even in Bacteria, Is Too Complex to Have Occurred by Chance" in Margenau and Varghese (eds.), Cosmos, Bios, Theos, p. 203)

"Scientists have no proof that life was not the result of an act of creation, but they are driven by the nature of their profession to seek explanations for the origin of life that lie within the boundaries of natural law. They ask themselves, "How did life arise out of inanimate matter? And what is the probability of that happening?" And to their chagrin they have no clear-cut answer, because chemists have never succeeded in reproducing nature's experiments on the creation of life out of nonliving matter. Scientists do not know how that happened, and furthermore, they do not know the chance of its happening. Perhaps the chance is very small, and the appearance of life on a planet is an event of miraculously low probability. Perhaps life on the earth is unique in this Universe. No scientific evidence precludes that possibility." (Jastrow, Robert, The Enchanted Loom: Mind In the Universe, 1981, p. 19)

"A five million year old piece of bone that was thought to be the collarbone of a humanlike creature is actually part of a dolphin rib... The problem with a lot of anthropologists is that they want so much to find a hominid that any scrap of bone becomes a hominid bone." (Dr. Tim White, anthropologist, University of California, Berkeley, New Scientist, April 28, 1983)

"One is forced to conclude that many scientists and technologists pay lip-service to Darwinian theory only because it supposedly excludes a Creator." (Dr. Michael Walker, Senior Lecturer in Anthropology, Sydney University, quoted in Quadrant, October, 1982)

"The irony is devastating. The main purpose of Darwinism was to drive every last trace of an incredible God from biology. But the theory replaces God with an even more incredible deity - omnipotent chance." (T. Rosazak, "Unfinished Animal," 1975, pp. 101-102)

Index Card 1

Focus 1

The Beginning of the Universe
(Space, time, matter, and energy)

Claim: The universe started with an explosion.

Lead-in question:
"Do you believe in the Big Bang?"

Front

Focus 1

The Beginning of the Universe
(Space, time, matter, and energy)

Dismantling Questions:
- *"Scientifically, can you have an explosion without energy?"*
- *"If there was no matter, what exploded?"*
- *"Scientifically, can something come from nothing?"*

Back

Index Card 2

The Beginning of the Universe
(Space, time, matter, and energy)

Claim: The universe started with an explosion.

Some believe matter and energy have always existed.

Front

The Beginning of the Universe
(Space, time, matter, and energy)

Dismantling Questions:
- *"Doesn't the second law of thermodynamics state that matter and energy are both deteriorating?"*
- *"How could matter and energy always have existed?"*
- *"Why haven't they already reached maximum decay?"*

Back

Index Card 3

Focus 2

The Beginning of Life

Claim: Life came from non-life. (Matter or chemicals)

Lead-in questions:
"What about the beginning of life itself?"
"Can life scientifically come from non-life?"

Front

Focus 2

The Beginning of Life

Dismantling Questions:
- *"Isn't Biogenesis a law of science?"* (Life only comes from other life)
- *"Is abiogenesis (Life from non life) scientific?"* (Has it ever been observed?)
- *If chemical evolution isn't happening today, how do we know it happened in the past?*

Back

Index Card 4

Focus 3

The Mechanisms for Evolution
(Mutations and natural selection)

Claim: Mutations and Natural Selection are the mechanisms that make evolution work.

Transition question:
"Have you ever thought about how evolution is supposed to work? Through mutations and natural selection."

Front

Focus 3

The Mechanisms for Evolution
(Mutations and natural selection)

Dismantling Questions:
- *"Aren't mutations almost always harmful?"*
- *"Don't mutations usually cause a net loss of information?"*
- *"Wouldn't mutations usually be the least likely to survive?"*

Back

Index Card 5

Focus 4

The Fossil Record

Claim: The fossil record proves evolution.

Lead-in question:
"Do you believe the fossil record proves evolution?"

Front

Focus 4

The Fossil Record

Dismantling Questions:
- *"Is the actual fossil evidence anything like the chart?"*
- *"What about the absence of transitional fossils?"*
- *"Are there any fossils clearly in transition?"*

Back

Index Card 6

There are three basic scientific reasons
I reject the theory of evolution:
1. The laws of science are in disagreement with it.
- *The first and second laws of thermodynamics*
- *The law of biogenesis*
- *The law of cause and effect*

2. The two mechanisms actually work against it.

3. I believe there is a better answer for the fossil record that fits the evidence better. Castastrophism, like the scientists in the mid-1800s believed.

I think I know why so many still believe in it though.

Front

You want to know why I think most people believe in evolution, and reject creation?

They are afraid if creation is true, they will have to stand before God and be judged some day. Did you know that isn't something people have to be afraid of?

What if I could show you how to take the fear out of dying and future judgment? Would you be interested?

(This is where you switch to the other simple plan, the simple plan of salvation that you feel most comfortable with.)

Back